THE POTTY BOOT CAMP: BASIC TRAINING FOR TODDLERS

SUZANNE RIFFEL

A MESSAGE FROM THE AUTHOR

Thanks again for your purchase and good luck. You are about to embark upon a challenging but ultimately incredibly rewarding phase in your toddler's development.

I want you to know that I am here to help. I truly want to know how the program works for you – both the ups and the downs. One unique feature of The Potty Boot Camp is that it is ever-evolving based on the feedback I have received from parents like yourself.

Contact me at Suzanne@ThePottyBootCamp.com

Visit our website at http://www.ThePottyBootCamp.com . You'll find potty training tips, advice, humorous tidbits, and useful products.

In addition, *please* send me a picture of your toddler after they are a proud potty graduate! No personal information is given - just first name and age.

Finally, don't forget to print out your child's graduation certificate. You can find it on the 'Graduates' page of our web site.

Warmly,

Suzanne Riffel

CONTENTS

CHAPTER ONE: THE POTTY BOOT CAMP

Whether you are ready to toilet train your eighteen month old or your three year old, you are about to embark on a frustrating yet ultimately rewarding phase of your child's development. I toilet trained my daughter at twenty months. At the time, I did not really think this was anything miraculous (and still do not.) Surprisingly, however, other moms that I met thought it was! I was constantly amazed at all the comments I received such as, "Wow! Is your daughter potty trained? How old is she?!?" The most common thing I was asked was, "How did you do that???" I decided to write it all down and pass along my program for potty training, which I now call "The Potty Boot Camp."

Although I encourage early potty training (before age two), the program works well for children eighteen months and older. The entire process will take three to four weeks; however, 90% of the training will occur in just one day! Your child will go from diapers to underwear overnight, and the following days and weeks are just follow-up intended to reinforce what they have learned. Think – In a matter of weeks, your child will be diaper free and reliably using the potty!

I would like to make a disclaimer. I am not a professional potty trainer - I am an eye doctor and a mom. If you get a sharp poke in the eye, I can help – my training covers that!

One thing I discovered, however, while potty training my daughter, is that there were certainly days I would have preferred being poked in the eye. It would have been easier than the entire potty process. It would have been easier than the entire potty process. I wish someone had provided me with a very specific, "how-to" manual so that I did not have to experiment or feel so lost while going through the process. I have, I believe, figured out a fairly quick and easy way to potty train your child. It worked for us, and I hope that it will work for you as well.

My goal with this book is to help other moms who are struggling the way I did when deciding how to potty train my daughter.

Here is what I found during my research:

1. There were many books about training - all of which were hundreds of pages long. I personally do not have time to read anything longer than "Goodnight Moon". This book is short – on purpose.
2. There was a lot of theory and very little how-to.
3. Many websites and publications promise a guarantee. I am sorry, but life makes no guarantees. Those claims made me suspicious.
4. There is too much conflicting information. Train early, train late, let the child self-train. My head was spinning.
5. As much as I would like to believe it possible, I concluded there is no easy or miraculous potty training method.

In the end, I did not find what I was looking for, which was a short, to- the-point, "cookbook-style" approach to potty training, and one without a lot of psychology. I wanted a flowchart or checklist that I could easily follow. After filtering through all of the information, I did find that I liked various aspects of each method I researched, and therefore my final training procedure is a combination of four of the most common toilet training techniques.

I am not naïve enough or arrogant enough to think my method will work for everyone. It did work for me, but I am hoping that each of you will e-mail me with feedback about how this program worked for you and your child. A unique feature of The Potty Boot Camp is that it is consistently evolving based on questions and feedback that I have received from parents like you.

CHAPTER TWO: THE POTTY BOOT CAMP CONCEPT

If you have done much research about toilet training, you probably have heard of the "Train in a Day" method, the "Naked and $75" method, the "Timer Method", and more. The concept behind The Potty Boot Camp is to combine the best of the best potty training methods.

Summarized below are some of the most common and well-known techniques:

"The Train in a Day" Method

The "Train in a Day" Method was first made popular back in the 1970s by the authors Azrin/Foxx in a book entitled "Toilet Training in Less Than a Day." More recently, Dr. Phil and Narmin Parpia have endorsed this training method. The basic premise of this technique is to go "cold-turkey" with diapers. One morning you announce to your child that they will no longer wear diapers. The child spends the next four to eight hours learning proper use of the toilet.

During those four to eight hours, your child learns how to use the toilet by playing with and teaching a doll proper use of the potty. The toddler receives positive reinforcement when successful and negative enforcement when there is an accident. The negative reinforcement involves "toileting drills." Positive reinforcement consists of rewards, a "potty party" and/or a "super hero" phone call.

"The Timer Method" of Toilet Training

The timer method is a technique considered by many parents to be less stressful for both parent and child than the "train in a day" method, however can take weeks to months to be successful. The parent sets a timer for pre-determined intervals. When the timer rings, the child is taken to the toilet for a potty session. If the child is successful, a reward such as a sticker is given. There is no negative reinforcement for accidents. As potty skills become more reliable, the interval between timer settings becomes longer.

This method can be difficult if you have a particularly stubborn child. Keeping motivational levels high for an extended period of time - enough time for the child to "catch on" - can be challenging.

"The Naked and $75" Method

The Naked and $75 method is the training technique endorsed by Dr. John Rosemond. Dr. Rosemond believes that toilet training should be simple and no-nonsense. The children are empowered to train themselves.

Training begins with an explanation of how and what is expected of the child. Parents show by example and explanation, and then tell their children, "Now it's your turn. Mommy and Daddy expect you to use the potty from now on." The child is naked for three to seven days while they learn how to use the toilet. The premise behind having the child be naked is to help to teach awareness of bodily function. (It is much easier for a child to realize they are pooping and peeing when it is running down their leg rather than having it land in an absorbent diaper.) The parent or caregiver is there to provide assistance if needed, but remains hands-off during the training process. (The $75 is for the inevitable carpet-cleaning bill!)

"Child-Centered" Toilet Training

Child centered potty training puts the child in charge of when and how to train. Many parents use this method with older kids (Two and a half or older) who have decided on their own that it is time to get rid of diapers. This is one of the most common trends in potty training children today. Children who have reached this decision on their own might be easy to train, however the disadvantage is that for many other children the "habit" of using diapers has become so ingrained that convincing them otherwise is very difficult. Late potty training can interfere with a child's admittance into preschool or participation in various activities. In addition, diaper usage typically costs parents an average of $1000.00 per year. Coincidentally, the introduction of "Child-centered" potty training coincided with the invention of disposable diapers. Prior to that time, diaper wearing meant diaper washing! Parents had much more incentive to toilet train early rather than leaving timing up to their toddler.

"The Potty Boot Camp"

With my training method, your child will train in four phases: Prep Work, "Boot Camp", Reinforcement, and Maintenance. Not all children are the same, so it is unrealistic to think that any one potty training method will work for every child. With The Potty Boot Camp, if your child just is not "getting it" during one phase, they will most likely catch on as you move on to the next. The

THE POTTY BOOT CAMP

Potty Boot Camp: Basic Training for Toddlers is brief by design. Parents of toddlers are incredibly busy, and most of us have little time to sit and read. Please forgive the lack of any "filler" material that would serve no useful purpose except to sell you a book with more paper!

Chapter Three: Psychology and Timing

When to Begin Training

When to train is probably one of the most widely debated child rearing issues. I am not about to get into that argument. I do not know the answer, so I will tell you what worked for us. My general opinion is the earlier the better. Human nature is such that the longer a bad habit becomes ingrained; the harder the habit is to break. When you give it some thought, which would be more difficult? Trying to stop smoking after three months of smoking, or after 10 years? I am certainly not saying that using diapers is a "bad habit". It is an absolute necessity. The longer your child is accustomed to using them, however, the harder it will be to stop.

If you are a parent of an older child (two and half or older), do not despair! The Potty Boot Camp works well for older toddlers as well. Later in the book, I will discuss various "motivational" techniques that can assist with a stubborn and opinionated youngster.

For those of you with children younger than two and a half, read on. For parents of older toddlers, skip ahead a few paragraphs to the section entitled "Are You and Your Child Ready?"

The Secret of Potty Training Before Age 2

Many parents ask for my "secret" that allowed me to train my daughter at twenty months. I have to tell them that no magic is required - the big "secret" to training before the age of two *is to train before the age of two!* Use common sense, though. As a parent, have you not noticed your child becoming more stubborn, independent, and opinionated, as they get older? Have you noticed your sweet little baby turning into a little person with his or her own agenda? I am guessing you are going to say yes. Now imagine your child a year from now. (You know the old saying "You ain't seen nothin' yet!") In general, your 18 to 26 month old child is going to be much more willing to please, much more willing to cooperate, and therefore much more willing to learn how to use the potty. Time after time, when a parent reports to me that their child is refusing to use the potty it is in a child who is closer to two and a half or older. "The Terrible Twos" acquired their reputation for a reason.

Another strong argument for early potty training is to look at historical data. Do you know that the average age of toilet training has increased every single decade for the past sixty years? Here are some truly amazing statistics: On average, in the 1940s children began training at four or five months! In 1946, Dr. Spock published his famous child-rearing book that discussed *waiting* until children could sit up at seven to nine months. At the time, this was a scandalous and shocking concept! In 1957, 92% of children were toilet trained by eighteen months. Human biology has not changed - just societal norms. I am amazed when I read articles or "tips" about "waiting" until your child is "ready" - even if that means waiting until age three or four. Do you think your grandmother waited until your mother was "ready" before getting rid of those diapers? Back then, when diaper wearing meant diaper cleaning, kids were toilet trained early. It is obviously physically possible.

If you have done much research about potty training so far, you will be familiar with the name Dr. Brazelton. In 1961, Dr. Brazelton completed a study that concluded that parents should delay toilet training until the child is ready. He emphasizes a "child-centered" approach where the child takes the lead. This is the most commonly cited study you will read about today and it is the reason for the swing toward late training. Here is the catch – Proctor and Gamble commissioned and paid for Dr. Brazelton's study. Proctor and Gamble just happened to manufacture the first disposable diaper! Obviously, the diaper industry and Dr. Brazelton had financial incentive to come to this conclusion.

I am sure that I will find many experts who will argue with me until they are blue in the face about the idea of training early. I am just a mom like you, who relies on intuition and good old common sense. Training early worked for me, and it has worked for millions of other parents as well.

Are You and Your Child Ready?

Here are the main questions to ask yourself in deciding if your child is ready.

1. Can he or she go two to three hours with a dry diaper?
2. Can your child respond to basic commands?
3. Are either you or your child able to tell when he or she is about to urinate or poop?
4. Can your child say "pee pee" or "poop" or whatever words you would like to use in your home?

Most importantly, do *you* think your child is ready? You are the best judge. You've got that "Mommy" (or Daddy) intuition".

Deep down inside, I think you know if your child is capable and ready to train.

What is the Definition of "Potty Trained?"

Here is another topic that stirs up violently opposing views: What is the true definition of "potty trained?" Is a child potty trained only when they can recognize the urge, go to the potty, pull down their pants unassisted, wipe, empty the potty bowl into the toilet, flush, and wash their hands - *all without any assistance?* On the far other end of the spectrum, is a child potty trained if the parent always gives reminders to go, takes the child to the potty, assists in all aspects of the process, and performs any necessary cleanup? Is a toddler toilet trained only when they have no accidents or when they are not wearing a diaper at night?

This is a decision you will need to make on your own. If you are hoping for scenario number one, – the unassisted version – you might be setting yourself up for a letdown.

I encourage parents to think of potty training as a skill that a child learns just as they learn the skill of walking. Think back to when your child first took their first wobbly steps. Their gait was awkward, their balance was off, and they took many falls. As the parent, you picked them back up again, kissed their boo-boos, and sent them on their way. Before you knew it, your child was walking up and down stairs, running, hopping, and skipping. The basic skill and concept was there from the beginning – it just required a lot of practice and refinement. The same is true for potty training. In the beginning, you might need to help your child quite a bit. Depending on the child, there might be accidents – *for days, for weeks, or even for months.* Do not get discouraged! It only gets easier and easier over time. In

BASIC TRAINING FOR TODDLERS

summary, I believe a child is "potty trained" if they understand the concept, know the basic mechanics, and use the potty *more often than not.* When at least ninety percent of pees land in the potty instead of on the floor you have succeeded!

Now, let us get started!

CHAPTER FOUR: PREP TIME – "ENLISTMENT"

The longer you spend completing this step, the better. I started prep work as soon as my child learned how to walk. Start these activities as early as possible – even as early as 12 months old! If you are reading this and are ready to train now, try to do these activities for at least one to two weeks. I began discussing pottying with my daughter the moment she began to walk. She had about six months of "prep time" - she knew how to wipe, how to flush, knew where pee and poop comes from, and had no fear of the toilet.

The goal of prep time is to make the potty a completely normal part of your child's day. The mechanics of using the toilet will not seem unfamiliar or foreign when you begin The Boot Camp day #1.

Prep Time Activities:

1. Take the child to the toilet two or three times per day while bare-bottomed. I did this at diaper changes. If you encounter resistance, or fear, start this step with the child clothed.
2. Have "playtime" on the potty. Read, sing songs, play with their favorite toy, etc. Do this as long as the child will sit there, which might be 30 seconds to 15 minutes, depending on their mood! If they happen to pee or poop, cheer and congratulate the child.
3. Let your child follow family members into the toilet. In a very matter-of-fact tone, explain what you are doing, where it is coming from, how-to wipe, etc.

4. Let the child watch contents of the toilet flush. Have the child flush if physically capable. Wave "bye-bye" to the pee or poop.
5. Buy one or two potty videos and let the child frequently watch them.
6. Read a toilet training book to the child regularly. My pediatrician recommended *Once Upon a Potty* by Alona Frankel.
7. Let child use his/her potty as a toy or a chair. This is to encourage familiarity and discourage fear of the toilet.
8. Buy a doll that pees and/or poops. Explain what the doll is doing, and why. You do not need to spend a lot of money on the doll – this is a useful tool but certainly not critical to your child's ultimate success. Many parents have success by just "pretending" with a favorite stuffed animal.
9. Teach the difference between "wet" versus "dry." This *is the most important concept you can pass along to your child before beginning potty training!* It is difficult to reward children for dry pants if they do not understand what the term "dry pants" means.

Congratulations! Now you just need to convince the child to actually put THEIR pee and poop in the potty.....which leads us to the actual training program....The Potty Boot Camp.

Chapter Five: "The Potty Boot Camp": Basic Training for Toddlers

The intensive "training" of your child's Potty Boot Camp takes place in the first few days....although you should be aware that reinforcement and maintenance might need to take place for days, weeks, and months to come. Before discussing training details, I would like to take a short detour into a topic that ultimately can affect your training success.

Actions versus Words

As you are toilet training your child, you will want to pay particular attention to your body language, tone, and choice of words. Keep in mind that what you *do* is as important as what you *say*.

Make your facial expression exaggerated and made to match the concept you are trying to convey. You will want to become an award winning actor! For example, let us say that you would like to teach your child that wet underpants are undesirable. To convey this concept, you will want to use a word (such as "icky") and you will want to *act* like are you are dealing with road kill! Pick up the underwear with the tips of your fingers, hold it out at arm's length, make a face as if you are smelling skunk, and act like you cannot wait to put them down. When you wish to convey that accidents are undesirable, make a sad face and pretend as if you are about to cry.

Keep in mind that toddlers do not understand subtleties of tone and expression like adults do.

BOOT CAMP: DAY #1

Day #1 is a modified version of the *Toilet Training in Less Than One Day* method taught by Nathan Azrin, PhD and Richard Foxx, Ph.D. Narmin Parpia in *Potty Training in One Day* writes another version of the "train in a day" theory. Dr. Phil also bases his training program on the train in a day concept. The primary purpose of day #1 is to set expectations for your child and to convince them that pee and poop belong in the potty. Today your child will give up diapers forever!

Go to the store and stock up on lots of "bribes" and "rewards" – small toys, candy, new videos, etc. The rewards will be used to celebrate having dry pants and potty successes. The bribes are to encourage motivation and cooperation as the day progresses. In addition, one of the keys to day one is to have your child drink many fluids....so purchase "special" drinks they normally cannot have. Many parents have written to me that they are opposed to bribes and/or junk food. Please keep in mind that I recommend these for only a few days. For now, getting the job done is your first priority. **(Refer to the shopping list in Appendix B.)**

I personally picked a day when just my child and I could be home together. Minimize distractions from other family members. Do not plan to leave the house and prepare yourself to miss a few phone calls. Dress your child in easy to pull down pants and *non-waterproof training pants*. (Yes, you will have to clean up some messes.) The waterproof training pants are padded and thick, and feel too much like diapers to the child. You might want to train in a non-carpeted area.

Allow four to five hours for training, and start right after breakfast. Sit down with your child and calmly explain that from now on, they are going to be a "big boy" or "big girl." No longer will they wear diapers. Explain firmly that pee and poop go into the potty, and not into their pants. Also, explain that you expect them to keep their new panties/underpants dry, and that you will now begin practicing going to the potty.

The following steps are summarized in a flow chart in Appendix C. *You might want to tape it to a refrigerator or cabinet so that you can easily refer to it throughout the day.*

Day One Procedure:

1. Take the child to the potty. If they can pull down their own pants, have them do so. If not, do it for them. Eventually they will learn to do it on their own, and in the meantime, it is not a big deal for you to help.
2. Get the child to sit as long as possible, for up to five minutes. If they happen to pee or poop, cheer wildly.
   a. Do not *force* your child to stay seated, but do everything you can to try to complete the five minutes. This will increase your chance of success.
   b. If your child "accidentally" goes in the potty during this first sitting session, do not give a reward other than verbal praise. You will want to give rewards today only for dry pants and purposeful pees in the toilet.
3. Set a timer for 10 minutes.
4. Feed the child drinks. Play quietly. Do not turn on the TV – yet. You might need that later in the day as a motivator.

THE POTTY BOOT CAMP

5. When the timer rings, check the child's pants. If they are dry, clap, cheer, and tell them how happy you are that they are keeping their panties or undies dry. Give a "small" reward.
6. Go sit on the potty again. Make it a game and as much fun as possible. Try for another five minutes. Get up.
7. Return to step #3.
8. At some point, your child will have an accident. When they do, calmly but firmly talk about how pee and poop go in the potty and not in their pants. Tell them you are sad they peed or pooped in their pants. Perform the "Cleanup" Procedure. **(See Appendix A, Cleanup Procedure)**
9. Now you get to be the drill sergeant - "Drill time!" Explain to the child that they now have to practice going to the potty. Take your child by the hand, walk to another room, and walk briskly back to the potty….all the while talking about needing to practice since they had an accident.
10. Walk to the potty, pull down their pants, have them sit down, and immediately pull up their pants. Walk to another room, walk back to the potty, and repeat. Do this ten times. Your child will probably be ok with this the first few times, and then might become angry. Be firm. Do it even with crying or complaining. Keep explaining that you are doing drills to practice because of their accident.
11. When done, go back to Step #3.

Keep repeating these steps for the next few hours. I found that my daughter started getting pretty bored with the whole process after about an hour. That is when I broke out the bribes. To get her to sit on the potty, I offered TV (she could only watch when sitting on the potty), candy, chips, soda....whatever it took to get her to sit. The TV worked the best – when she knew she could only watch Barney when on the potty, it was a strong motivator to stay put. The second she got up, the TV went off. Find your child's "currency" – the activity or item that will maintain their interest. You can let them play with a forbidden household object they have been dying to get their hands on. Try for "newness" – as we all know, a brand new toy, book, snack food, or video will maintain a child's attention much longer than something familiar will.

At some point during all of this, you will have a success while sitting on the potty! Make a very big deal of this – Give big hugs and lots of praise. Bring out a "medium" reward.

Now you can relax – a bit. Return to step #3, but his time set the timer for 20-minute intervals. If they have an accident, return to step #8.

After about four hours, try to have your child take a nap. By the end of the four hours, your child will likely be getting mad and or upset about the practice drills. The way my daughter was carrying on toward the end made me feel like a terrible mother! Some parents have told me that they find the drills too "traumatic" or "harsh." For the drills to be successful, you need to be firm. Remain calm and matter-of-fact. Remember your tone of voice and mannerisms. Try not to let any frustration show. If your child senses you becoming distressed or upset, you will likely not succeed. That said, some people simply do not have it in them to make their child upset. If this is the case, use your parenting common sense to set limits to the drills. Stop them completely if your child is having a complete meltdown, or try to do five drills instead of ten. Day 1 will only be successful if you are consistent and follow-through. Hang in there! Narmin Parpia says to continue these drills past the first day. I do not think it is necessary. Trust me; you will have made your point.

Most likely, sometime toward the end of the day, perhaps after their nap, your child will tell you they have to pee – or even walk over to the potty all on their own! This is a significant moment...trust me, you will feel like you have conquered Mt. Everest. My daughter had the "big moment" late in the evening – do not get discouraged. We gave my daughter "THE big reward" (in our case, it was a tricycle) for initiating herself. That way she knew she had truly accomplished something special.

When Day One Doesn't Go as Planned

Ninety percent of children will self-initiate by the end of day one – but one in ten will not. Do not get discouraged if you are in this group. Below are a few possible scenarios:

1. Your child has not had any accidents and thus has not had enough opportunity to do practice drills.
2. Your child did many drills and potty-sitting practice sessions but never had any successes. (Self-initiated or otherwise.)
3. Your child had success on the potty during the sitting sessions but never self-initiated.

If one of these scenarios applies to you, follow these steps:
1. Do another half day of drills with the following modifications: (Repeat day one for another three to four hours.)

a. If your child *had a lot of accidents* but *no successes*, change the timing of the technique. Instead of five minutes on the potty and ten minutes off, do one minute on the potty and five minutes off.

b. If your child *did not have many accidents* but also *has had no successes*, do twenty minutes off the potty and two to three minutes on the potty.

c. If your child *had a few accidents and at least one success*, continue the same timing pattern as day number one.

2. Continue cleanup technique.
3. Reduce drills to one or two repetitions only.

At this point, you will find yourself in one of two situations:

1. Your child finally "got it" and self-initiated.
2. Your child still has not self-initiated.

If your find your situation is the former, congratulations! If you are in situation number two, you will have a couple of decisions to make. If you think you can mentally handle another couple of days of accidents, go ahead and begin day number two. (Naked intervals.) If you are to the point you do not think you can take it anymore, you can begin either using waterproof training pants (padded) or pull-up style diapers *with underwear underneath.* (This allows for the sensation of wetness.) Keep in mind that your training might ultimately take longer to complete if you do this – but ultimately you will still succeed!

DAYS #2-4 "NAKED INTERVALS" (REINFORCEMENT)

Your child now fully understands what you expect of him or her. It is now time to let them habitually use the potty and reinforce what they have learned.

Keep your child bare-bottomed for the next few days for two reasons:

1. It is easier for the child to get to the potty in time.
2. I took the advice of John Rosemond, who touts the "Naked and $75" method. According to Dr. Rosemond, children HATE the feeling of having bodily fluids running down their legs. I found this to be true.

There might be a few messes. Try hard NOT to ask your child every five minutes "Do you have to pee?" You want the child to take responsibility for his own actions. On the other hand, the child is likely not trained enough to reliably tell you every time they have to go to the potty. You will have to provide some gentle reminders.

You likely will have your child in diapers at naptime or bedtime. If your child routinely wakes up dry from naps, discontinue the diaper for naps. If your child can routinely wake up in the morning with dry diapers, discontinue the diaper for bedtime. This will probably not be the case unless the child is over 2 ½ years old. Just explain to your child that the diapers (or pull-ons) are "only for bedtime and will help to keep you dry!" The book *A Potty For Me: A Lift-The-Flap Instruction Manual*, by Karen Katz, reinforces this concept nicely.

*****The best product on the market for the interval phase of training is the Potty Watch by Potty Time Inc. I love the Potty

Watch because *toddlers* love the Potty Watch. For some reason, when a parent tells a child to use the potty a very common response is "NO!" The Potty Watch works so well because it is an "external" force telling your child to go to the potty. Children tend to argue less and be less defiant when some *"thing"* is directing their actions rather than their parent.

The procedure for "Naked Intervals" is as follows:

1. Set the timer for every 30 minutes. Have the child sit on the potty as long as they will tolerate. If they are resistant, again bring out the bribes. If they are successful, clap and cheer. Try not to provide rewards other than positive feedback. That said, if you need assistance in keeping motivation high, or if you are encountering resistance, you could certainly consider a potty training aid. Some of these include sticker charts or potty "advent" calendars. **(See Appendix B for a full list of helpful training products.)**
2. When they have an accident....and trust me; they will, they will likely stop and call for help.
3. Calmly, firmly, and with a tone of disapproval in your voice, remind your child that pee and poop go in the potty. Have the child clean up as much as they are capable of doing so. **(Again refer to Appendix A, "Cleanup Procedure")**
4. Return to step #1 but each day try to increase the timer by 10 to 15 minutes.

***Side note: Regarding leaving the house: During waking hours, try hard not to put a diaper on your child. Bring along a portable potty everywhere you go. I would recommend an incredible product called the "On The Go Potty" by Kalencom. The product is a travel potty that easily fits into your diaper bag or purse.

DAYS #5 AND ON: "GRADUATION"

Obviously, your child cannot run around without underwear or bottoms forever. The next step is to return to underwear. Go to the store and let the child pick out their own panties/underpants – it will make them more excited about wearing them. Although I describe day five as the beginning of "graduation," you can certainly move on to this phase earlier if your child is a pottying star! If by day two or three your toddler is having few to no accidents, feel free to move ahead!

The procedure:

1. Stop using the timer. Tell your child that they have "graduated" from Potty Boot Camp and now get to wear their new underwear!
2. Verbally remind and/or ask your child about every 45 minutes to an hour if they need to use the potty. A hint in making this work is to make a statement such as "It's time to go potty" rather than asking a question. "Do you have to go potty?" is almost certainly going to get you a reply of "No!"

When there is a problem during the "graduation" phase, it tends to be in children who do great when they are naked but have accidents the minute they begin to wear underwear. My theory on this complication is that when your child feels the material it re-awakens "bladder memory" of wearing a diaper. Should you

26

have this dilemma, do not stop using the timer. Continue to use your timer or potty watch while wearing underwear, and continue to do so until you have achieved few to no accidents. At that time, you can discontinue the timer and move on to verbal reminders.

CHAPTER SIX: "MAINTENANCE PHASE"

The maintenance phase starts when your child is having only a few sporadic accidents. Here is the good news: Your child is potty trained! The bad news: You are in potty reminder maintenance mode, which in many ways is more difficult than the initial training! The moment you let up, your child is likely to regress…so be vigilant!

Handling Maintenance: Remind, remind, remind. Ask your child if they have to go upon waking, after lunch, after a nap, after a car ride, when arriving at a store, *before* going to the park, *after* going to the park……you get my drift. I stopped asking/coaxing/pleading with my daughter and figured I would always let her tell ME when she needed to go which was the wrong decision! No sooner had I done that then she started having accidents again. Younger children tend to be less consistent about telling you when they need to go compared to older toddlers. As your child grows, you will find his or her reliability improving.

When you get the occasional accident, always firmly remind the child that pee and poop go in the potty, and that you are disappointed that they went in their pants. Most likely, the child will be just as upset about the incident as you are!

Chapter Seven: The Stubborn Child

Imagine this scenario: You complete Day #1 successfully. Your child is 90% trained! Day #2 goes well also. Day #3 arrives, and suddenly your toddler shouts a vehement "NO!" whenever it is time to use the potty. What do you do?

Stubborn children can be the biggest obstacle to potty training success. I jokingly say that parents sometimes have to perform "criminal acts" in order to achieve the desired goal. A combination of positive reinforcement ("bribes") and negative reinforcement ("extortion") will often work wonders for your child's motivational levels.

Using too much bribery can ultimately backfire because the child might become accustomed to rewards and begin to expect them. On the other hand, using only negative reinforcement can cause a stubborn child only to become more stubborn. I recommend mixing it up so the child does not know what is coming next – a treat or an undesired consequence. Below are just a few ideas you can use to try to encourage cooperation:

"Bribes" – Extortion:

Enthusiasm, potty training products (appendix B), a special activity (play with Mom's purse), a trip to a restaurant or museum, snacks or candy, new toys or trinkets, TV privileges, or coins/money.

"Extortion" – Negative Consequences

Cleanup technique (always use), take away privileges (TV, toy, Etc.), quiet time ("No TV/Toy/Etc until you use the potty"), or withhold snacks ("No dessert today!) Another technique parents

THE POTTY BOOT CAMP

can try is the "Merit/Demerit" Technique. The merit/demerit technique combines both positive and negative reinforcement. To use this method, go to the store and buy about 10 small toys. (Examples are matchbox cars for boys or princess figurines for girls.) The toys need not cost much, but try to find items your child will consider special.

Take the toys and line them up on a shelf in a location where your child can see them but not reach them. Sit down with your toddler and have a conversation about the merit/demerit technique. Explain that you will be playing a new game. Show her the toys and explain that she will get a new toy every time she uses the potty. If, however, she has an accident she will have to put the toy back on the shelf. Make a big deal of success – "Hooray! You get a pee-pee toy! Let's go pick one out!" You will also want to make a big deal about taking it away. (As always, perform cleanup first.) "Oh, I'm so sad! You had an accident and now you have to give up your special new toy." Make the child go find the last toy they received and give it to you. Have a sad "bye bye toy" ceremony. "Poor Megan, I'm so sad you have to put your toy back. Unfortunately, those are the rules. Say "bye bye" to the toy. Wave to the toy, and then place it back up on the shelf. Remind your child that the next time he uses the potty can get the toy back or even pick out a new one.

Hopefully, the temptation of wanting the toy back will entice your child to use the potty the next time.

You can also use this technique on a smaller scale with items like coins, backyard rocks, or books. Find and use any trinket or item your child likes to hoard, collect, or play with.

Chapter Eight: The Potty "Poop Camp"

This chapter applies to children who have graduated the basic potty training course but who are having difficulty having bowel movements in the toilet. Most parents can skip this chapter. You can always refer back to it later on if needed.

A question parents ask me on a regular basis is "Why won't my child poop on the potty?" Know that you are not alone if currently facing this common toilet training problem. As frustrating as it might be, you can take steps to help overcome this obstacle to diaper freedom.

More common in older potty training children (2.5 years and older), the "poop" issue can become a major power struggle between you and your toddler. Causes of this apparent stubbornness might be fear, medical problems, embarrassment, or standard toddler contrariness. Let us tackle each issue one by one.

Medical Problems:
First, a disclaimer: If you believe your child's unwillingness to poop on the potty is truly a medical issue, please consult with your pediatrician. Chronic constipation can cause a medical condition called encopresis. Children experiencing encopresis have a problem with the bowel that dulls the normal senses about the urge to go. A more benign medical condition is basic constipation, in which the child fails to have a bowel movement over a couple of days. Usually an increase in dietary fiber or a mild stool softener will help to relieve the situation.

Fear:

Unbelievably, many children believe that poop is a part of their body. Imagine how reluctant you might be to use the toilet if you thought a body part might fall off each time! For other children, the fear comes from the actual sensation of air hitting their bottom, the "plop" that can be heard in the water below, or the sound of flushing. Other children have had a previous painful episode of constipation and they become afraid to experience it again.

Embarrassment:

I think many of us can confess to occasionally "making a stink" about our child's poop. We joke or tease about the smell, or the size, or the consistency of the poop. Some children, especially the "sensitive" ones, can become self-conscious about this bodily function. If you think this might be the reason for your child's problem, try to discuss poop in a very matter-of-fact manner. Make it clear to your child that pooping is a very normal and natural part of life. It might be helpful to read books to your child such as "Everyone Poops" by Taro Gomi.

Stubbornness:

For most parents reading this article, the "terrible twos (or threes, or fours)" might be the culprit in your potty problems. The key in convincing your child to use the toilet rather than their pants is to find a method to make the child finally decide that life is just easier and more sanitary if they use the toilet. Some parents are violently opposed to bribes or "punishment" but sometimes the basic concept of "you get as good as you give" is the magic answer. If you child cooperates, they get positive reinforcement. If they do not, the child receives negative reinforcement.

Allowing the child to decide if the positives outweigh the negatives will actually empower them and allow for increased independence. It is also temporary – believe me, you will not have to bribe your child to poop in the potty on the day of their high school graduation!

A Method to End the Madness

Assuming that you find yourself in the "stubbornness" category above, the "Potty Boot Camp Pooping Program" is outlined below.

Step #1

If you think fear of poop falling might be the issue, make sure you are using a child's potty. Then stuff the collection bowl full of toilet paper. That way when the child sits down they will feel the "cushioning" against their rear (more like a diaper), which might help them to feel more comfortable "letting go."

Step #2

Make the child do as much of the cleanup as they are physically capable of completing. **(Refer to Appendix A, "Cleanup Technique")** Do not act angry, or frustrated. Simply tell them that pooping in their pants is completely unacceptable. You want to make the whole clean-up process seem like something "yucky." Exaggerate your facial expressions when you are touching the underwear, keep making little noises such as "ewwwh, this is sooo gross." Act like the underpants or panties are contaminated with nuclear waste. Tell your child "You pooped in your pants. Now you need to clean yourself up." Try to make it clear to your child that the *poop* is not disgusting – it is the poop *in the pants* that makes it so "yucky".

Make the child walk to the bathroom with the poop in their pants. Have him pull the underwear down, pick them up, and put the poop into the toilet. Then get some wipes and make them wipe themselves up. (Yes, it is likely the poop will get onto his legs and/or the floor – grit your teeth and hang in there!) Keep supervising - "Yes, that's good. Oh - you missed a spot right there." You get the idea. Then have your child actually carry the underwear over to the sink, turn on the water, and make them "wash" the underwear. (You might need to help the first time.) Your son or daughter will soon figure out that pooping in their pants is more trouble than it is worth.

Step #3

If "cleaning up" is not convincing enough, you can do a trick I call the "Poopy Present Box". Get a large box, or bag. Go out and buy about 25 small "presents." It can be anything - little cars, books, etc - nothing too big. Put the box up somewhere where your child cannot see inside it. Then explain to them that the box is their "poopy present box." Every time he or she goes poop in the potty, they get a present from the box. Be firm - absolutely no looking into the box or getting presents unless there is poop in the potty! Then, do not say another word. Try hard to not discuss the topic, or pressure them to use the toilet for poop. Let the child decide on their own that the desire for presents is more important than using their underwear as a toilet. Continue to do the cleanup routine when they do not use the potty. By the time they get through the entire present box, pooping in the potty is usually such a routine part of their day that they will eventually just go without expecting something in return. Should that not be the case, make the presents in the box progressively less interesting as time goes by.

Step #4

I am hoping that most of you have succeeded by now – but here is the next step in the program should it be needed. The fourth thing you can do is to take away presents if the child has an accident. This is a tactic reserved for the most stubborn children. If he or she poops in their underwear, go through the cleanup process and then find the last "present" they received from the box. Show your child the present, ask them if they remember why they got the present, and explain that those presents are only for kids who use the toilet. Make your child take the present over to the box and throw it in. Tell them you are very sorry and that you really want them to have the present -- but it is out of your control. "Those are the Poopy present box rules." Let your child know they can have it back the next time they poop in the toilet.

Step #5 – For the Desperate!

Step #5 is your last resort - use this only when you cannot even get your child to poop on the potty *even once.*

Desperate Technique #1:

Find an item that is very important to them - a favorite stuffed animal, etc...and put it into the present box until they use the toilet. Make sure you get down to your child's level. Look them in the eye and explain why you are taking away their favorite item. Make it clear that this makes you very, very sad. Explain that they will get the item back as soon as they poop in the potty. Most of the time you will find the child will use the potty rather quickly. However, you might mentally prepare yourself for a number of hours with a very unhappy toddler.

Desperate Technique #2:

I refer to this technique as "poop jail." I first read about the method from Dr. John Rosemond, whose opinions I generally respect. Tell your toddler that you spoke with doctor today and the doctor told you that it is time to use the potty for poop. Explain that the doctor said your child must go into the bathroom and stay there until he poops. Place your child in the bathroom, gate them in, and explain that the doctor said they could come out and play as soon as they poop. Be very nonchalant and matter of fact. Do not act as if you feel badly about "trapping" the toddler in the bathroom. Use a tone of voice similar to one you would use to discuss the weather. Then tell your child, "Ok, I'm going to be in the other room! Call me when you have pooped. Bye! See you in a little bit!" Then leave. Resist the urge to check in on your child and do not respond to complaining. Most parents report to me that this technique works in less than a few hours. Surprisingly, I also hear that most children *do not* cry or become upset!

Both of the "desperate" techniques feel "mean" to me, but again use these only as a last resort. If these methods make you uncomfortable, or if they do not work, you might want to stop potty training for a while.

CHAPTER NINE: REGRESSION

Regression is common for a number of reasons. Many parents report to me that the birth of a sibling brings about regression. Other children will do great for months and then will suddenly stop using the potty. Some children like all the attention they received early on in the training process and simply miss it. You will also want to rule out any medical problems such as a bladder infection.

If your child has a few "bad days" and has three or four accidents per day, try to ride it out. If, however, the accidents continue into the third or fourth day you can assume your child has regressed. In this case, perform the following steps until your child is back on track. Most of the time the toddler has not forgotten what to do – she simply does not want to!

. Below is the regression procedure:

1. Resume timed intervals. Use your Potty Watch or timer and set the device for thirty to sixty minute intervals.

2. If after one or two days you do not have success using the timer, try decreasing the timer intervals. (For example, use fifteen-minute periods instead of thirty.)

3. Try the "merit/demerit" technique as previously described earlier in the book. Continue to use the timer.

4. If after a number of days the above steps do not seem to be effective, I recommend resuming the same drills that you used back on Day #1.

41

Summary

That is it....it is a lot of work but very rewarding for everyone involved. You will be amazed at how happy and full of pride your child will be when they "do it" on their own. My little girl to this day says, "Mommy! Look! Pee-Pee!" and then runs over for her "pee pee hug." You will be instilling self-confidence and self-reliance into your child, which are characteristics that will carry with them throughout their lives.

APPENDIX A: CLEANUP PROCEDURE

Cleanup Procedure

Throughout The Potty Boot Camp, there is one task I will ask you consistently and repeatedly to perform with your child. This is the "Cleanup Procedure." Cleaning up makes your child responsible for their accidents and reinforces that actions have consequences.

For the most part, the cleanup technique is self-explanatory. You will want to make your child do as much of the cleanup after an accident as they are physically able to do. As I have discussed earlier in the book, your actions and words are key to making this successful. When your child has an accident, you will want to make a statement such as, "Oh my! You had an accident! My gosh, now you have to clean yourself up. Accidents are no fun, are they? Stop playing for a while and let us go clean up."

Try to stand back and supervise. For younger toddlers, resist the urge to help pull down pants or wipe the floor. Stay near the child and simply explain every step. "Ok, let's first clean the floor. Go get some towels. Let us walk back to the accident. Now wipe up the pee pee with the towel. Good! Oh – Look, you missed a spot!" Make this process take as long as possible. For older children, show them the correct procedure the first time they have an accident and thereafter make them do *everything*. (Leave the room if possible.)

Next, show the child how to and change their clothes. Have them pull down their pants and walk to the sink. Take the dirty underwear and "wash" them. Put them in the laundry.

Now your child will need to clean herself up. Hop into the bathtub, run the water, and "wash off". (I know I do not need to tell you always to supervise your child in the bathtub!) Dry off, and then go get clean underwear and bottoms. If your toddler is old enough to put on their own clothes, have them also complete this step.

The key to the cleanup technique is to make this such a chore that your child decides it is easier to use the potty. Do not make it fun, and try not to have a lot of conversation with your toddler other than what is required to communicate what they are to do next. If you can leave the room the technique becomes that much more effective because now the child is not only performing a chore – they are missing whatever fun is taking place in the next room!

APPENDIX B: SHOPPING LIST

Prep Time

Child's Training Potty
Toilet Seat Insert
Doll that simulates urination
Books about potty training (recommendations only) *Once Upon a Potty* by Alona Frankel *A Potty For Me: A Lift-the-Flap Instruction Manual* by Karen Katz *The Potty Dance* Personalized Book
Videos about potty training

Basic Training

Potty Watch and/or Portable Kitchen Timer
Beverages your child will consider a "treat", i.e. Soda, Fruit Punch, etc.
Salty Snacks (to hopefully induce thirst)
Small Rewards (10 to 15), such as party favors, candy, etc.
Non-waterproof training pants (5 or 6 pairs.)
"Medium" sized reward such as new video, small toy, etc. (suggestion only)
"The Big Reward" such as new wagon, ride-on-toy, etc. (suggestion only)

Graduation and Maintenance
New panties/underwear (10 or 15) (Involve child in selection)
Portable potty such as the by *On the Go Potty®* by Potette® or *Caboose Diaper Travel Potty*
Pull-on style diapers for nighttime use (if child under age 2 ½)
Training Pants (only if unable to continue "underwear only" outside the home) such as the *Trickle Free Trainer*
Potty Training Sticker Chart or Reward System such as Potty Training Rewards.com

Appendix C: Flowchart Boot Camp Day #1

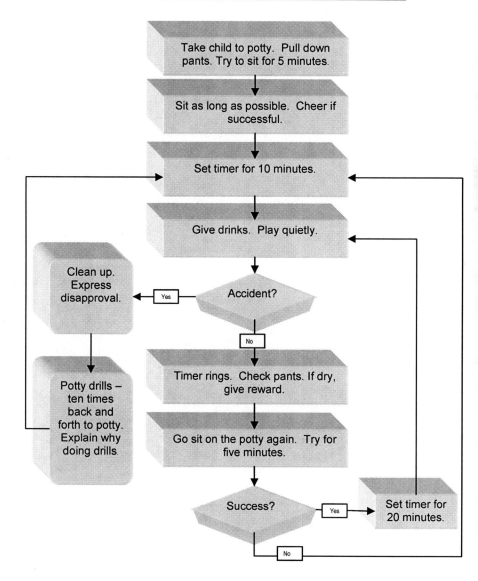

Take child to potty. Pull down pants. Try to sit for 5 minutes.

Sit as long as possible. Cheer if successful.

Set timer for 10 minutes.

Give drinks. Play quietly.

Clean up. Express disapproval. ◀— Yes — Accident?

No

Potty drills – ten times back and forth to potty. Explain why doing drills.

Timer rings. Check pants. If dry, give reward.

Go sit on the potty again. Try for five minutes.

Success? — Yes —▶ Set timer for 20 minutes.

No

CPSIA information can be obtained at www.ICGtesting.com
Printed in the USA
240771LV00003B/38/P

9 781601 455192